The Divine Flame

ELDER PORPHYRIOS

Lit in My Heart

MONK AGAPIOS

The Divine Flame ELDER PORPHYRIOS Lit in My Heart

2nd edition

PUBLICATIONS
THE TRANSFIGURATION OF THE SAVIOR

MILESSI 2013

In Greek *1st edition: Athens, November 1999*
2nd edition: Athens, December 1999
3rd edition: Athens, September 2000
4th edition: Athens, August 2000
5th edition: Athenes, April 2004
6th edition: Athens, December 2005
7th edition: Athens, June 2007
In English *1st edition: Athens, 2005*

Book title
in Greek: Ἡ θεϊκὴ φλόγα ποὺ ἄναψε στὴν καρδιά μου ὁ Γέρων Πορφύριος

Headquarters: 7 Araklovou str., GR-115 22, Athens, Greece
Metochi: Milessi, GR-190 15, Nea Palatia, Greece
Tel. (+30) 22950 98261, Fax: (+30) 22950 98074
email: info@porphyrios.gr
www.porphyrios.gr & www.porphyrios.net

ISBN-13: 9789606890246
ISBN-10: 9606890244

DTP: **PANEKTYPON PUBLICATIONS**
P.B. 70, GR- 72 100, Mardati, Ag. Nikolaos, Crete, Greece
Tel.- Fax (+30) 28410 26301, (+30) 697 2609572
email: info@panektypon.com, www.panektypon.com

CONTENTS

After My Admission Into the Monastery

Acknowledgements

We are deeply indebted to the esteemed Fr. C. J. Simones who first had the inspiration and the initiative to translate this book with the cooperation of rev. Fr. Nick Pallis. We offer them our heartfelt thanks for all their love and hard work. We are especially grateful to all those who read the manuscript and benefited us with their helpful criticism and advice. The final version is the result of their contribution.

Kavsokalyvia

PROLOGUE

The text of this book was given to us by the monk Agapios a little while after the venerable repose of Elder Porphyrios. For various reasons, we suppressed our love for Elder Porphyrios and as in the case of various other similar texts, we did not publish it. However, the constant requests of friends and colleagues that we publish all material gathered about Elder Porphyrios overcame our reservations. And thus, with this book, we begin slowly to publish all such information for the benefit of pious Christians and for the glory of God. For a better understanding of the text, we are adding footnotes.

For those of you who are reading about Elder Porphyrios for the first time, we wish to inform you that he was a priest-monk. He was born in Evia, Greece in 1906. As a child of 12 or 14 years of age, he went to the Holy Mountain (Mount Athos) and practiced asceticism at Kavsokalyvia (one of the many monastic communities on Mt. Athos). While at this Monastery he became very sick and his elders sent him to a monastery outside the Holy Mountain to recover. He, in fact, recovered, and at the age of 20 they ordained him to the priesthood, in spite of his objections because he thought he did not deserve it. Until 1940, he remained in the monasteries of Evia. In 1940 he was appointed as the chaplain of the Polyclinic Hospital in Omonoia Square, in Athens, Greece. He served in this capacity for 33 years. The last few years of this time period, he lived also at St. Nicholas church, in Kallisia, Penteli. In 1981 he founded the Convent of the Transfiguration of the Savior, his dependency at Milessi. In June of 1991, he departed for the Monastery of Kavsokalyvia on the Holy Mountain where he fell asleep venerably on December 2nd.

His spiritual contribution to the world have been presented within many books and articles in the Greek language. These books and articles have also been translated in other languages. From all these books, our Monastery has published the following:

Kl. Ioannides, *"Elder Porphyrios", Witnesses and Experiences,* 315 pages, 7th edition, also in English and in Romanian as well.

Const. Yiannitsiotis, *"Near Elder Porphyrios"*, 498 pages, 2nd edition, also in Romanian and soon to be translated into English.

Anth. Tzavara, *"Recollections of Elder Porphyrios"*, 190 pages, 8th edition, also in Romanian.

Anarg. Kalliatsou, *"Father Porphyrios"*, 220 pages, 4th edition, also in Russian, and Romanian and soon to be translated in English.

The main characteristics of Elder Porphyrios were his humility, love, knowledge of God and the many gifts of the Holy Spirit, such as clairvoyance (discernment), prayer, and healings. With such gifts, he helped and continues to help, even after his repose, those who call upon him. We humbly ask him to intercede to the Lord to forgive our many sins, and above all, to forgive us for the delay in offering our faithful brethren the material that we have collected about his spiritual and philanthropic gifts. We feel that, up to this moment, we have hidden the light "under the bushel" and we must now place it upon the lamp-stand so that it may shine upon everyone.

The Holy Convent of the
Transfiguration of the Savior

Milessi 10/18/99
The Feast Day of the Commemoration
of St. Luke the Evangelist

The First Meeting

"A simple monk... with tranquility and natural meekness, he responded to everyone"

Through the prayers of our Holy Elder Porphyrios
may whatever I write be for the glory of The Living God,
Who glorifies those who glorify Him.

How I Met The Elder For The First Time

Ilways had the desire to meet a holy person, to see how he lives. One afternoon, friends of mine took me to a monastery in Milessi. These people knew the Elder well. They wanted me to meet a man such as is rarely found in our times.

I first saw him sitting in an automobile, next to the driver. They had just brought him back from a visit to another place. I did not take my eyes off him for a moment. I was scrutinizing him closely. There were many other people who were waiting for him.

I noted how simply and humbly he behaved. I was impressed how he came out of the car and greeted people. From time to time he would say spontaneously almost within himself, "Lord..." or "Lord Jesus Christ...".

There was nothing pretentious or ostentatious about him. He was a simple monk. People were telling him different things and he responded to everyone with calmness and meekness.

I kept looking at him. Sometimes he would look at me as he was speaking to other people.

He appeared to me just like Christ amongst the multitude of His people.

The people who took me there introduced me to the Elder:

"Our brother here works nearby and we brought him here to meet you."

"Elder, may I have your blessing", I asked. "I rejoice to be in your presence and I would rejoice even more if I had the opportunity to speak with you."

"I humbly desire this in the name of the Lord. Do you want us to meet tomorrow morning?", he asked.

"I gladly accept, early, early in the morning, 7... 7:30.", I replied.

"I will be waiting for you. Go with the blessing of God." As he blessed me on the head I kissed his hand.

I left with a feeling that I never felt before. I felt great inward joy. I was flying. My heart was enthralled and I continually repeated what the Elder said: "Lord Jesus Christ..."

I had also heard from other Spiritual Fathers that we should say the Prayer of Jesus but I could not get my lips to say it. I felt that it was like a commandment that was imposed from without and I had not managed to implement it.

Now, without realizing it, my heart had been ignited by a divine flame. With love and gratitude I was proclaiming to God what my eyes had seen and what my ears had heard while in the presence of that Elder monk.

I had prepared what I would say and early the next morning I went to Milessi. There was a shed there and a little trailer home that was parked amongst the fir trees. This place looked more beautiful in the light of day.

I stood apart from the thirteen morning visitors who had arrived before me and were waiting for the Elder.

The Elder came out and directed his attention toward me. "Let's go for a walk in that direction".

"Elder, I just came. Those other people came before me."

"Listen to me, let us go. I know those other people."

We proceeded to an open area where some newly planted fruit bearing trees had begun to blossom.

"This is my first walk here. Because of the cold weather and my sickness, it has been six months since I have been outdoors," he said.

He enjoyed nature like a little child. He walked lightly and every now and then he whispered spontaneously, "Lord Jesus Christ".

I wondered why he didn't say the whole prayer as they teach us to do but he said only half of it?

Am I Smart or Foolish?

I began simply and spontaneously opening my heart to him and asking him whatever was of concern to me.

"Elder, I want to become a monk. I love the monastic life. I desire to live for Christ. I visit a monastery but everything has become confusing for me and I have many questions. Please tell me, must a monk be smart or foolish?

"I ask this question because whatever I do they constantly scold me and tell me that a monk doesn't have a personality and that here things are not as you have known them but as you find them and as they tell you. A monk cannot have his own opinion or speak back to his elders.

"On the contrary, other people who have achieved something are praised for it. They tell them that they succeeded because they are bright. They succeed at all things. They are considered bright. So, I am confused."

The Elder responded, "A person who gives his heart to Christ, like a Monk, becomes another person. His mind opens up. It is filled with Christ. Do you hear me? Do you understand me? When your mind and heart are filled with Christ then you are wise and smart and the Spirit of God teaches you everything.

"The word smart, is not meant in the way people understand it; in other words a person responds by putting another person down or by doing a job better than others. But that is all it is! How can I explain it to you?

"In every difficult situation that arises a truly smart person does not lose control of himself, is not at a loss. He does not despair but takes refuge in Christ, Who is within him. He finds nice and easy ways to overcome his problems. He does this without being upset or by suffering inner turmoil. Do you understand George?" (He said my name without ever asking me what my name was. Neither did they tell him my name yesterday when I was introduced to him. That impressed me).

"I understand, Elder."

He continued, "The person who has given his heart to Christ doesn't suffer no matter how many difficulties he encounters. He rejoices, he is filled with inner joy. He is creative. He is careful. He does not make mistakes or harm anyone. His mind, his hands, and his feet, all move by the Grace of God. How is it possible for him to be foolish?

"Of course there are circumstances when he must act foolish for the sake of Christ. "How will he pretend to be foolish?".

"When he keeps silent, he does this knowingly from within himself He acts as if he doesn't understand. He pretends that he does not know because of some inner determination. He pretends not to understand. He pretends he doesn't know because he has a better purpose in mind. These things will be taught to him very slowly by the Holy Spirit. This is so because when we have Christ in us, we live in a way that we ourselves do not determine. When Christ lives in us, He determines our life."

The Wisdom of Christ. Here is an example the Elder shared with me

We didn't have an abundance of water at the monastery. In fact, we had a limited supply. They wanted to dig a long ditch in order to bring in the needed water".

I said, "Your effort is in vain. The ditch will get blocked up and we will be without water. Let us install pipes."

"But the expense is great", they said.

"We will do it right and it will last. We purchased good-sized pipes and we directed the water right into the Monastery. Everyone rejoiced and glorified God.

There you have it, the Spirit of God gives inventiveness to the mind of man to do what is best."

The Love of Christ and Prayer

I said to the Elder, "They are constantly saying prayers at the monastery. They are always saying the Jesus prayer. While at their various chores they recite supplications and salutations. They do this for whole hours at a time. After this they go to the Church for services.

"I can't stand it any more. My mind has become tired. I feel that I am about to burst. But nevertheless I want to become a monk. What will I do? Help me."

The Elder said, "A young girl used to come here and confess her sins. She was in her second grade of Junior High School. She told me once, 'Father, I have fallen in love with a boy and I can't get him out of my mind. My mind is constantly on him, on Nick. One would think that Nick is here, (she pointed with her finger to her forehead). I begin to read and Nick is here. I go to eat and to sleep but nothing changes. Nick is here. What can I do father?'"

"My child," I told her, "you are still young. Be patient, finish school and then Nick will still be here. Now you must put effort into your lessons. A week passed and she came again."

"Dear Father, it's impossible for me to concentrate on my lessons. Constantly all day long my mind and my heart are on Nick. Nick has become an obsession with me and it won't go away."

(As he was saying these things, I was thinking, "What connection do these things have with me? Maybe he is telling me these things to give me a respite from my obsession.")

The Elder continued, (while reading my thoughts) "you are now saying, why is he telling me these things?"

"But nevertheless, tell me, please."

"Did this girl sit on a stool?[1] Did she force herself to focus her mind on Nick? No.

"This happened spontaneously. This was unforced love.

"The same happens with us. When we love Christ with divine love, without any coercion, pressure or worry, with love we will proclaim His holy name, 'Lord Jesus Christ.'

"And when the heart is flooded by this divine love, it does not require us to verbalize the whole prayer, 'Lord Jesus Christ, have mercy on me.'

Before he finishes the prayer the heart stops at that point out of love and rejoicing.

Other times he proclaims only the "Lord..." and stops. He proclaims this mystically and without speaking."

In saying these things he gave me an answer to my

[1] Here the Elder was referring to the low stool which is recommended by certain fathers for whomever wishes to do mental prayer. The meaning of his word is: Did this girl make any effort?

first question that was not expressed verbally. I had only thought it without verbalizing it.

I was flabbergasted. I was totally amazed at his responses. A divine flame enveloped my inner being and I felt the desire to begin proclaiming within my heart the ineffable love I had for the name of our Christ.

Instructive Recollections From the Holy Mountain

Subsequently, the Elder related to me some things from his life on the Mountain that were relevant to our topic.

"I lived a heavenly life on the Mountain. I was about twelve years old when I went there. I had two Elders and I was totally obedient to them. They sent me to fetch two bags of dirt for their gardens. This work had to be done by noon. I ran barefoot, jumping among the rocks.

My hair was not combed and I shouted in the wilderness, 'O Spotless, Undefiled, Incorrupt, Immaculate...', 'Lord Jesus Christ, have mercy on me' and other hymns which I was memorizing from the '*Parakletike*' and from the '*Menaion*'. If someone by chance would have seen me, they would most likely have said, 'That monk has gone crazy'.

And truly, divine eros is a type of holy madness which overwhelms a man and changes him in body and soul. Do you believe this?"

"Certainly, Elder, since you are saying it, I believe it."

"What I tell you is what I saw happen to myself.

"My soul was changed by my love for Christ. Even my face was changed. I say this because one day as I was running again with divine zeal to carry out the chores that had been entrusted to me I accidentally saw by chance the reflection of my face in a glass. And I was astounded to see how my life in Christ, which I was living on the Mountain, had enhanced my external appearance. This is spoken about in Holy Scripture, 'a gladdened heart makes a cheerful countenance.'[2]

"And you, George, love Christ and you will see that all those changes will take place within you. Give your heart to Christ and everything else will become His work."

After the encounter

I lived this miracle for about one hour. On returning home, and upon leaving the Elder, felt as if I was descending from Mount Tabor.

I was ecstatic and I tried very hard to bring myself back to reality. I was returning home and to my work. From then on I was drawn to the Elder like a magnet.

I thirsted to learn all the secrets of monastic life. It is quite different reading about it in the Patristic books

[2] It is from the book of Proverbs of the Old Testament (chapter 15 verse 13).

and quite something else hearing about it from someone who has lived the life himself.

As soon as I returned home from the Elder, I immediately made notes of everything he had told me. And when we spoke on the telephone, I carefully wrote down everything he said so that I would not miss any of his holy words.

My thoughts had focused on God and my daily concern was and is to be totally obedient to Him.

Treasures
From Our Subsequent Conversations

Some Other Things He Told Me About His Life on the Mountain

One day, I arrived at his little trailer home about two to two-thirty in the afternoon.

"Welcome. How is it that you arrived here at this time of day? Is there another person outside?"

"No, I'm the last one. I have come to find out from you how we can acquire the Grace of God."

"I was in obedience to two elders on the Holy Mountain. They were strict. They scolded me. They never praised me. However I felt their love.

"I occupied myself with woodcarving. But they would not let me complete the whole job. You will do the job up to this point but no further," they said.

"(I didn't know why they did this to me. I now realise that others who had learned the whole job probably left after learning)."

A Handicraft Without Question

Once both Elders were absent. I saw a little bird nibbling on the grapes on the vine. I immediately took a piece of wood and carved that particular scene. It was beautiful. It was like a living bird with its wings unfurled and the grape looked real. As soon as the Elder returned I showed him with a great sense of joy what I had done."

"What is this?" he said to me. "Where did you get

"I love them. I want to help all of them, but I can't"

permission to do this?" He immediately proceeded to break it into two pieces."

"My, my! Didn't you get upset, Elder?"

"I didn't get upset because I realized that I should have asked for permission."

I immediately silently scolded myself.

"I, Elder, I have great difficulty in asking for permission. When I am in the monastery, I prefer not to do something rather than to humble myself by asking for permission."

And the Elder responded: "I lived a heavenly life at the monastery because I didn't do anything on my own. I was constantly asking. You know the monastic life is not a life that is free, quiet, and carefree. It is a life that is pressured by humility and submission. It is one thing to desire to become a monk and something else to be made for monasticism. In other words, if someone does not set out with profound love for Christ, he is apt to go crazy. Do you understand these things that I am telling you?"

"Certainly, Elder, I think that I understand you."

"Man, in his primitive and wild state lived alone. He did whatever he wanted. The roots of wildness exist within us. Many people, especially women, seek isolation so that they can be free from submission to their parents. They want to live alone to live as they desire to live. This is not the monastic life.

"People go to the monastery with these primitive elements of wildness that prevailed in primitive man. And as soon as the struggle begins, when the requirements for obedience and dependence are imposed, they get frustrated and say, *They don't understand me,* and then they leave. They end up finding themselves alone with their own will. These things happen more frequently to women".

How Grace Comes

"God sends His Grace to the man who submits himself to Him and asks for It. In order for Grace to come we need humility and *certain patterns of behavior are necessary from us.*"

"Which mannerisms? What do you mean?"

"I don't know if I should tell it to you. It's not proper. Something is written about this in the works of St. Isaac the Syrian." He retrieved a book from the shelf and leafed through the pages. He was having a difficult time saying it and finding it. At one point he said, "Lord Jesus Christ" and opening the book forcefully, he immediately found what he was looking for.

He read the text: "He who reached the love of God no longer desires to remain here. This happened because love negates fear. My beloved, because I have become a fool, I cannot bear to keep this mystery a secret. I become a fool for the benefit of my brothers because this true love cannot be kept secret from people you love. Many times when I was writing these things my fingers remained motionless on the paper and I could not bear the joy that overwhelmed my heart and calmed my feelings." [1]

The Elder read to me up to here. And this meant to me "I am telling you ineffable things out of love. I too am becoming a fool "for the welfare of my brothers, as Abba Isaac did".

And furthermore while Abba Isaac was writing, "his heart was opening up to Christ and he stood still" and his fingers remained motionless on the paper.

Subsequently, so that I could understand, since I asked him twice, he related the following to me:

[1] The title of the book is: The Revealed Ascetical Writings the Excerpts from the 38 homilies.

What happened to Him at Saint John the Theologian Monastery on Patmos

"One summer, when I was in Athens, a dentist friend of mine and his wife asked me if we could go to the Monastery of Saint John the Theologian on Patmos.

"We went to the cave where the Revelations were received. The very spot where the rock was ripped open, where Saint John lay down and where he grabbed the rock to get up.

"You should know that these places have become sanctified. They impart holiness and grace.

"I felt my heart opening up little by little and then I walked out because there were other people there. In the afternoon, wanting to once again live this grace, I asked that we go there again. I told my companions to remain bowed and motionless while saying the prayer. 'Don't get up and don't be concerned about anything that you might see.'

"I also bowed and was saying the prayer. But the Grace would not come as it had that morning. I got up and censed the altar, and the whole Church. I came back to my place and then my heart opened up. I remained with my hands open for a long time.

"My soul was filled to overflowing. Only one person entered and probably saw me. I

don't know. It probably was the parish priest and he left again. We got up and kept silent until the evening. I didn't eat much. They never asked me anything. I told them not to discuss what happened because it's not proper. It is something that can be easily misunderstood. This is the proper way. I did not force myself. I did not become upset. I did not get impatient. I got up, I censed, and the Grace came of its own accord, when It wanted to come. And you should keep your mind on profound things: "Lord Jesus Christ..." Allow yourself to be loose and unhurried in the hands of God and He will come and envelope your soul."

When I Told Him I Was Definitively Leaving for the Monastery

When I told him that I was definitely leaving for the Monastery and that in a few days they would tonsure me, he leapt for joy. On that day he spoke to me and advised me extensively! In the end, when we were bidding each other farewell, he naturally took my hand and kissed it. I, living the mystery that surrounded me, asked myself what meaning did this have. Then he said to me:

"Do you see what I just did?"

"Certainly, you kissed my hand, the hand of the wretched and unworthy one." I responded.

"Therefore, you must know that with your tonsure Christ will embrace you. He will kiss you and you will become His own. He will become your own.

"Our Christ makes your soul his Bride forever, for all eternity.

"Know that I will pray for you because I love you a lot. Your soul is sensitive and has all the good dispositions to love Christ a lot, as one ought.

"It is such souls that Christ wants for His Brides.

"If you love Christ with all the strength of your heart, everything will be easy for you. Even obedience and humility will be easy. Then your love for all the brothers will be love unforced and spontaneous. It is the same love that Christ has because it will not be you who loves but Christ Himself Who now possesses your heart."

Love temptations

The Elder told me, "Pay attention to only one thing. Clarify your thoughts that are pressured and grieved by your sensitive personality. Banish them away so they don't remain with you. Love the temptations[2] which come to you and you will not be agitated nor will you be grieved.

[2] The *advice to love the temptations* seems strange, because every day we pray as follows: *and lead us not into temptation.* However the Fathers distinguish between voluntary and involuntary temptation or between temptations of sin and temptations of affliction. They teach that the Lord's Prayer refers only to the voluntary ones or the temptations of sin. Whereas as regards the involuntary ones or the temptations of afflictions the James writes in his Catholic Epistle. *"My brethren, count it all joy when you fall into various trials, knowing that the testing of your faith produces patience. But let patience have its perfect work, that you may be perfect and complete, lacking nothing."* (James 1: 2-4). In other words, have great joy, my brethren, when you fall into various afflictions because you must know that the trial of your faith (which occurs within afflictions) creates patience. Let your patience have a perfect work so that you may be perfect. Let your work be complete without you lacking in anything (spiritual). See Abba Isaac, Homily 44 *"For he who flees*

"Love exceedingly all the brothers equally. Love the Elder very much for an Elder is like Christ".

"How can I love the temptations and the difficulties?", I asked.

"This is an important issue. It has its ways. "If Christ enters your heart He fills it with His love. When this happens an ambivalent attitude cannot exist such as

temptations, flees virtue. While temptation I say not of desires, but of afflictions." See also Maximus, the Confessor, the chapters on Theology, the fifth hundred §63. Philokalia of the Neptics Fathers, vol. 2, page 145, ed. Aster (in Greek).

"While the Lord on the one hand teaches us to pray against voluntary temptations, like the delight of the flesh which causes pain to the soul. While the Great James, speaking on involuntary sins urges us to rejoice in our temptations, as taking away the delight of the flesh. " In other words, while the Lord teaches us to ask to be delivered of our voluntary temptations because they bring delight to the body and pain to the soul, the Great James urges us to rejoice in our involuntary temptations, which take away delight from the body on the one hand and pain *from* the soul on the other hand. So it is obvious that the Elder Porphyrios is referring to the temptations of afflictions. In general, the Fathers urge patience with temptations. See for example the saying of Saint Anthony in the Gerontikon. "*Take away temptations and no one will be saved*" (Ed. Aster by P. V. Paschos, page 1 in Greek). See also Abba Dorotheos, Practical Teaching on the Christian Life, Translation, introduction and glossary by Const. Scouteris, Athens 2000, page 205 §141. *Temptations greatly benefit those who bear them with courage. For even though passion bothers us, we ought not to be disturbed by this.* In other words, temptations greatly benefit those who bear them with patience. Even a temptation which aims to stir up our passions, should not be allowed to upset.

don't do this or don't do that. Only love prevails, above all Love[3].

"The negatives existed before the advent of Christ. Christ abolished them. He brought Love to replace it. The life of Christ is Paradise, obedience, and humility."

Why He left the Holy Mountain

"I told you that there on the Mountain I lived a Heavenly life."

"And why did you leave, Elder?"

"I did not leave, they expelled me."

"They expelled you? Why?"

"It is a long story. I was in constant motion. I did not stay put for one minute. I constantly created work for myself in order to push myself. I always did these things with permission.

"The one Elder would tell me to 'dig here'.

I would dig. The other Elder would come and say: 'why are you digging here'?

'Father Ioannikios told me to dig.'

'No, not here. Leave here and go there.'

[3] The meaning of the words of Elder Porphyrios is that the negative commandments, Thou shall not steal, thou shall not commit adultery, thou shall not bear false witness etc., had been given before Christ and they demanded implementation out of fear for God. After the Advent of Christ, however, the commandments are kept by Christians out of love. ("If you love me, you will keep my commandments" John 14: 15) and they are not abolished as some deceived people contend.

'Let it be blessed.' I would go.

Ioannikios would come and say,

'Hey you, what did I tell you? I sent you to this place I didn't tell you to go there?'

'Yes, but Fr. Panteleimon said here.'

'All right, continue.'

Others thought that they were very strict.

Few stayed with them. I obeyed them eagerly. I saw them as very good for me.

Now that I think about them, I must admit that they were strict.

I moved around barefoot in winter and summer.

We abstained from meat, eggs and cheese. We had strict fasting. I was very healthy from the age of twelve until I was nineteen.

One winter they sent me to fetch snails. Four hours I gathered them up in the snow.

I carried a wet sack on my back. It was like ice. I became ill with pleurisy.

We did not have good food and medicines.

I became skin and bones.

I told them that I would surely die. A brother monk had come from a long distance. He placed a blister plaster on my back. Do you know what a blister plaster is?"

"No, I don't know." I responded.

"It is a square piece of leather. They stick it on the back where the pleurisy is located. It gathers all the liquid from the pleurisy and becomes large like a bubble.

After about a week, they cut this piece of skin off with a pair of scissors. They also cut your flesh with it and it is dreadfully painful... As a result of the great pain, I chanted, *'Because of my many sins...'*.

"Afterwards they placed a bandage on the wound soaked in wax and other substances. This would gather up the pus and they would change the bandage. Every time they changed the bandage I suffered great pain.

"It was necessary for me to have good food so they sent me to Athens for one month. I would recover and return to the monastery. Again I would become ill. They then sent me to Athens for two months. The same thing happened. Upon my return, I got sick again.

"Finally after conferring about me, they decided to ask me to leave the monastery permanently.

"With many tears I bade them farewell.

"My monastic brother accompanied me to the boat. We both cried.

"My dear priest, don't cry," I told him, "I will come back again."

"My child, don't cry," he told me, "The Pan- aghia will bring you back."

"We said these things to console ourselves and we cried. This scene will remain unforgettable for me. I have great nostalgia for that heavenly life of obedience. My Elders were very good. Later on, when one of them fell asleep in the Lord, the other Elder strangely disappeared. They searched for him everywhere. Even the Police searched but they found nothing. We don't know what happened to the other one."

I Read A lot

I" read a lot. I was very studious. I read mystically. I took the time to do this whenever I could. I learned the Gospels of Matthew and Luke by heart and I learned half the Gospel of John. I also learned the Psalms. I studied the Fathers. I studied for many hours. I did spiritual work.

And you should know that I did not know how to read. I had only a second grade education in elementary school.

When I first went to the Monastery, during the vespers service, they gave me the Psalter to read.

I began syllabizing "Bless-ed- is-the-ma-n."

"All right," they told me, "that's enough." You will take the Psalter, you will read it well so you can learn it. You will also read the Synaxarion of the Saints. Nothing else. "I read but I didn't understand. I did not have dictionaries. For example, I did not know that *oikos* means home. Thus I would find the same word elsewhere and from the context I would find the meaning of the words. I memorized whole pieces and all day, as I ran amongst the rocks, I recited them loudly with emphasis. Later on, I took the *Paracletike,* the *Triodion,* and the *Menaion.* I read with passion."

As the Elder was saying all these things about his life, I felt he said them directly to me in order to urge me to do the same thing and much more with the help of God. I had learned a few things. I was not uneducated.

Having expressed himself in this way I became convinced and was amazed by his ability to read my soul and to enlighten all the dark areas of it. A bit later he added, “That which I liked most of everything was the Trinitarian canon every Sunday night at the Sunday Midnight Hours. When the brother read it, I became very attentive. And sometimes when he read softly or quickly and I didn't understand or did not hear properly I would get very upset. Then I would retreat into myself and would fall into the Jesus Prayer.”

Hearing these things, I would become very critical of myself. Because every time the Trinitarian canon was read, I would say within myself, “Oh! This is difficult. I don't understand it.” And until the reading was finished, I would purposely not pay attention. At that moment, I felt intellectual chaos reigned within me. What a wretch I was.”

I didn't interrupt him. I allowed him to add whatever he wanted.

My heart began to be enlightened as if this clairvoyant Elder was opening up a window in it. Near him, I felt an infinite sense of simplicity and trust. I believed without any doubt that he had received Grace from God to read our hearts and that he knew all of our secret passions and weaknesses.

And May You Experience Them All

The Elder continued, “And you, while you are there at the monastery, you must be very focused during the service. You are to follow them. You should experience them all. This includes the hours, the mid-hours, the psalms, and the canons. Don't allow one word to escape your attention. You are to read clearly and with meaning. We should proclaim with love and worship unto our Lord, 'Lord Jesus Christ have mercy on me.'

Do many prostrations. Do as many as are required of you. They purify and sanctify the body and the soul."

"From now on you will not be able to come here. Our communication will be spiritual. When you pray to our Panaghia seeking help every time you have a problem or some difficulty, you will say to her, 'Most Holy Theo-to- kos, through the prayers of the Elder, help me with such and such a problem.' And I will be informed of your problem and I will pray for you spiritually. I want to know the day and the hour that you will be tonsured because spiritually, I will also be there near you."

After My Admission Into the Monastery

The Little Horse of Saint George

As a monk, my communication with the Elder did not stop. He continued to guide me by telephone from his little cell in Milessi.

Once I told him, "When I was in the world I helped the poor a lot. Now I know people who are suffering and I can't help them and that worries me."

"Be careful," he warned, "I had suffered the same thing when I was on the Mountain. I wanted to help a friend of mine to come to the joy of the Mountain.

For one month my thoughts and my heart were focused on this issue. How could I find a way to bring him here? I lost my focus for prayer and peace. I told this to my spiritual father."

"You should have told me sooner," he told me. "The devil is bothering you." 'Tell me, who brought you here?"

"God, Father."

"This is therefore the issue. Pray a lot. Tell God about your friend. Tell St. George and he will bring your friend with his little horse. You should not worry. Entrust every person you love to God. I now answer you in the same way. You might send others to the Monastery but always with the blessing of your Elder."

You Will Suffer a Beating at the Hands of Haralambos

He told me once, "Let us love with the love of Christ and not with the love of humans. Two years ago a mother came here to tell me about her four children. She told me their names and I told her, 'Be careful about Haralambos because you will be beaten-up by him. (He was then twelve years old).

She became enraged. 'What are you saying, Father? Haralambos is my best child. I pay attention to him and I love him more than all because he is my youngest.'

I then responded, 'You don't love him with the love of Christ and you are therefore doing him harm.' She did not believe me. She left angry saying harsh things about me. I prayed and left her in the hands of God. She came to me the day before yesterday having repented. 'Forgive me, father. We misunderstood you then. We said you are deceiving the people. Now I believe that God enlightens you. Haralambos left me, dear Father. He's become like a wild animal. He beat me up. What can I do now? Truly I did not love him with the love of Christ. I did him harm' she cried.

And the Elder continued telling me, "In reference to your brother, if he wants to, let him come to the monastery. But on the other hand you should not keep constant company with him because you will do harm to him and to everyone else. Allow the Elder and the Brothers to help him. You should pray a lot for your whole brotherhood, for the whole Church. We are undergoing difficult days."

Give Yourself to Christ

I was worried and he counseled me. "Didn't I tell you on another occasion that when you completely open your heart to the Lord, without reservations, the Lord will enter it and make it incapable of sinning? Did you understand? You become incapable of evil. When the Lord loves us in the depths of our heart He brings meekness and kindness. Even if we wish to get angry, to do harm to other people, we are unable."

"Then the saying holds true 'I no longer live.' You live this and proclaim this within yourself. St. Paul was beside himself because of the great joy that he felt and he proclaimed it openly. But does Christ change? As He was then, so is He now...."

"My dear man, since we say these things and agree on them, why must we say the same things again after we fall victims to the same problems?

"Take it seriously and don't allow yourself to give satisfaction to the devil.

"Give yourself completely to Christ with fervent love and longing. When you see something and you inwardly become defensive about it and you try hard not to speak, you tighten up. In reacting this way, you are already in trouble by becoming defensive."

"Be simple, prudent, and focused. Always feel the presence of the Lord. He will teach you what to say and when to be silent."

Becoming a Missionary Without Speaking

"My dear man I am envious of you, I envy you. You can become the greatest missionary in the Monastery without speaking at all. You will pray for everyone in silence. You will pray for the whole Church, for the clergy, and for the Monks. Our Church is undergoing a crisis today.

"Above all pray for your spiritual family."

"Leave your heart completely open to Christ, filled with love, and filled with worship. If we do not do this, the Spirit of God abandons us. It leaves us when we ask why this or why that. Oh, if I were only young again like you so that I could live in obedience! There is no greater happiness than to do whatever they tell you to do and to immerse yourself in the love of God."

"*Prosilosis*[1]. Do you know what that means? It is (in greek) from the pros (towards) and ilos (nail). It means being nailed to that which you love. You should nail yourself to Christ."

"I love Christ very much and I believe in His power. My dear man, the Apostles would pass by and their shadows would heal the faithful. Isn't our Christ the same? Did He change? We have changed! What do anxiety, nervousness and psychiatric illnesses mean? I believe that the devil exists in all of these.

"We don't submit to Christ with love. The devil en-

[1] *Prosilosis* means undistracted concentration of the mind.

ters and mixes us up. Oh, if I could live like you! To be subservient in a monastery (in greek: coenobium!) I am envious of you! I love you very much in the name of Christ. And I want you to become a true monk."

Forgiveness

"There are monks who say forgive me. They confess this and yet inside there A still exists animosity against the other person. With this kind of attitude the Grace of God doesn't come to us."

"I had a craftsman working here. He was a neighbor, and he did various jobs and he was getting paid for his work. I don't know how it happened but he started bad-mouthing me to everyone, both here and elsewhere. I was saying to myself what can I do? How can I help him?"

"One day I went to his house for a visit. As soon as he saw me he lost control. He became defensive and turned yellow. He thought that I went there to scold him. I began telling him about his trees and that I was amazed at their abundant fruit. We spoke about hospitality. That was it. His heart began warming up. And from that moment, he never failed to come here and to do various jobs. In such cases a good way to handle someone is needed."

"Some time ago, they brought me a stationary bicycle so I could exercise in my cell. I also asked the cardiologist about it. He told me that it is good for my heart. I should exercise lightly. In the morning I wake up at about two or three o clock. My mind is clear and I pray.

Afterwards, instead of prostrations, I exercise on the stationary bicycle and constantly say the prayer."

Useful Counsels for All Monks

Y" ou can and must become a leader in the monastery without realizing it, without speaking. You can accomplish this only through fervent prayer for everyone. Open your heart simply, unforced, and spontaneously to our Lord.

"Don't force yourself, nor pressure yourself nor doubt that this will happen. In all this you should speak first to the Lord. And before you speak to your Elder, first pray fervently. A praying person, a simple monk with his prayer, can correct all the problems in the Monastery."

"Be pleasant. Love silence because your heart will be speaking to Christ. But when you meet your brother monk speak to him with love so that hearts can be connected. They must be as one. Don't respond with many words when someone asks you a question. You should answer with a few meaningful words. You should learn to respond with 'thank you' and 'please.'

It should be said with the meaning 'I thank God, whose angel sent you to help me.'[2]"

"I, however, as I had told you, went to the Mountain

[2] The Elder was not accustomed to saying *thank you* and *please* to fellow monastics. He preferred the expression *"bless* " and *"let it be blessed.* " Here he is obviously referring to specific cases respecting the composition of souls of the brothers. But in reference to the

at the age of 12 or 14 years. I was an uneducated and unlettered child. But my heart was filled with divine love. I responded to all the chores with eagerness. I did more than what they asked me to do."

"They never advised me. They never praised me as they do today with young children. We constantly say to our children 'well- done, well-done' and the poor things grow up all puffed up with egos. We do great harm to our children. My elders urged me to read only the Psalter and the Synaxari. They gave me nothing else in the form of counsel and guidance. I soared. I lived in Paradise. And I didn't get sick from excessive work but rather from egotism. My ego pushed me to gather as many snails as possible in the rain. The wet sack remained on my back for three hours."

"So you too should love physical effort and tiredness. It is good for the body and for the soul. My dear friend, I want you to be like me because I love you. I want you to become like me.[3] Do you do prostrations? How many do you do?

Just do one so that I can see how you do it."

This happened there, at Milessi, in his little cell,

thank you, he gives the meaning of thanksgiving to God and not to the brother.

3 Elder Porphyrios who was filled with grace and altered by the love of Christ lived his new life in Christ in an atmosphere of enthusiasm. His complete dedication to Christ in the footsteps of the Apostle Paul, led him effortlessly to the saving and urgent counsel of Paul: *"Become you imitators of me as I also am of Christ"*.

when I went one day as a monk. I did one or two prostrations.

"You don't do them right." And though he was now blind and could not see at all, nevertheless he spoke as if he could see.

He called a brother monk, ringing his little bell.

"Please show this brother monk how I taught you to do the prostrations and the rule."

And immediately he began doing prostrations vigorously.

"You see," the Elder said, "first the hands touch the ground, not the knees. And then the body remains as if it is in mid air. It demands strength in the arms. Then you cross yourself with firmness! You firmly touch your forehead, your knee and your shoulders! We at the skete, when we all did the Rule together in Church you could hear the rustling of our cassocks as the hand hit the knee with firmness. Have you seen how a mother squeezes her child?

"Human emotion is part of every action. This is also true with the Lord."

"At the time of practicing the Rule both the body and the soul should feel Him. That hermit that I saw praying did many-many prostrations and at certain moments he would be in ecstasy with his hands open and outstretched. This is the meaning of the expression, 'The Lord was troubled in spirit.'[4] At other times the hands softly and beseechingly supplicate the Lord."

[4] At a certain time the Elder particularly stressed the intensity of

"When we meet in prayer, you there and I here, you should feel mentally that we are gazing upon the Lord and the Panaghia. We should run to take refuge in Christ out of divine eros and love. We do this not out of fear of death or divine retribution. Death does not exist. Don't fear death. There is no death, for whoever dies with faith in Christ there is no death for that person. If you have not died, then die."[5]

The Quarrelsome Brother

I once told him, "Elder, I can't work together with this brother... he is a complainer." "You fool, you are an egotist. Do you know that? Because of this you suffer in many ways."

"I know it Elder. I have been like this from my youth. Pray that God will give me a humble heart."

"When the heart has God-given humility it sees everything clearly. It already lives in the earthly Uncreated Church of God. I am referring to humility that is not said with words, neither is it that which we feel we have acquired. Holy humility is a gift of God to the soul. God gives it when He finds pristine preparation. Then He

the Spirit of the Lord with the word "he was troubled in the spirit," which means he was completely shaken, like the neighing of a horse. He wanted to stress the completeness and perfection of the soul, mind and strength that had been given to Christ and to prayer, as if the believer wants something very strong in soul and body.

5 Spiritual death does NOT exist for a true Christian. The "die" is directed to the "old" man, i.e., die to the old man and put on Christ.

looks upon it with pleasure and draws this soul towards Himself. You should not say that your brother is obstinate, that he is jealous or that he gets angry etc. Don't say that I can't get along with him. I can't ever do things with him. This is not the way to act. This is not Orthodox. It is not Christian. This is not at all living in the love of God. This is the way to separate yourself from the Grace of God, because you separate Him from your brothers."

"On the contrary, you will overlook their weaknesses and without imitating them, you will become one with them in cooperation. You will accept whatever they want and the way they want it. Do they want it this way? So be it. Do they want it another way? May it be the other way. In this way, the walls that separate us from our brothers are destroyed. It is in this way that we are united with Christ."

"The more you are daily associated with your brothers, the more you mystically enter into the Love of Christ. 'Stand in freedom' says St. Paul."

"When I was young and I was secretly planning my departure for the Holy Mountain, I sat and thought of ways I would find olive oil to light the lantern, to acquire books and other things that are necessary for the ascetic way of life. And when I went there all these worries were resolved. Everything was taken care of."

Teaching By Example

In his attempt to help me he always connected me with events in his life on Mount Athos. He would at times give me examples from his daily life.

These examples were sometimes positive and sometimes negative.

He often interrupted the conversation and asked, "Did you understand this?"

"Certainly, Elder. With your blessing, I think I understood it. "

"Say it again, what did I tell you?"

I would repeat it. At other times he remained pleased and proceeded. At other times he was not pleased. "You didn't understand this. It contains a profound meaning. I must explain it to you."

My beloved father (Elder Porphyrios) had great love and great patience. I also had absolute trust in him and told him everything which burdened my soul. Whatever he told me was law for me. It was the will of God.

For this reason I wrote his words in my heart and in my notes. I would not tell anyone anything. He had told them to me verbally, putting his hand on his mouth.

"Whatever I tell you, I don't want you to repeat it anywhere. I say this because others who hear these things will not understand them. This is especially true of little old ladies. They will say 'you know we saw him levitating above the ground. He was standing half a meter above the ground. He is a saint.' Some will say he is a saint and others will say he is deluded and deceives the people with everything that he tells them."

“The ideal for all of us is to give ourselves totally to Christ with all our heart”

The Son of Disobedience Is a Product of Oppression

“A mother complained that her son no longer her, he doesn’t go to Church and the like. I told her, “You oppressed him for so many years. You ordered him around constantly. Now he wants freedom. Don’t order him around. Only pray with spiritual love for him. If you saw a Turk controlling your son and dictating to him to 'Say this or that thing to your mother,' would you blame your son? Would you blame your child? Of course not!"

Facing Discord with Prayer

"My friend, Christ said that we should love our enemies. Do you understand this? It is a great thing for us to love everyone and to pray for them. The devil bothered one of you. He made him uneasy and agitated. If the others are not ready to counter him with prayer, the disturbance is transmitted to everyone.

On the contrary, if one prays for others, the disturbance is limited. The Grace of God radiates and through this Grace it spreads throughout the whole environment and sanctifies it."

Divine Eros
Makes Prayer Imperative

A person was upset with his wife. At noontime, when he got tired at work, he asked himself where he should go. He went to Elli, his wife, to get some rest."

"Do you hear my child do you hear? He was very tired. He went to a certain place.

They talked and he rested. Because the flame of love was present, he found rest. This is a great thing."

"Do we have divine love for Christ?

"If we are exhausted, we should approach Him through prayer so that we can find rest.

"You said to me that you got tired during prayer and during the service. What is missing? Divine love is missing."

"How will we acquire it, Elder?"

"It is not dependent on our own efforts. It is a gift of God.

"He loves us first if we are pleasing to him. Our own attempts and external influences may bring about the opposite result to our souls: It may bring abhorrence towards spiritual things. And how will God love us? For God to love us something else is needed from us. This is it! We should humble ourselves. We should bow. We should love. We should pray. We should seek God."

"The responsibilities and the cares of life are not to blame." He said this as if he were reading my thoughts, that I had so many jobs and responsibilities that the time came and my mind could not bear it any longer.

"Listen so that you may be amazed!

"The other person was a female doctor! Didn't she have responsibilities in the office, in the Hospital and in the home? But nevertheless, she waited for the proper time after getting terribly tired to be near her beloved. Do you believe this? In that situation tiredness was overcome. Everything is overcome! Do you understand this?"

About Vigils

"You should love vigils. Vigils are very important. Do you understand this?

They are a very important thing. Heaven opens up. We speak with God.

"During our vigils up there, up until about midnight I would get a little drowsy My eyes would get very heavy. Afterwards my mind would open up and I lived in prayer until the morning. When it finished, I was so motivated that if there was a way for it to begin again from the beginning, I would have welcomed it. In the skete we read the canon[6] clearly and with meaning. When the vigils took place in the Kyriakon, [trans-note: Main Church] we chanted it."

Elder, I Get Angry

One day I told the Elder, "Elder I get angry. Lately I get angry easily." "Anger is a good thing." I thought he was joking and I interrupted him.

"A good thing?"

"Certainly. God put anger inside us. It is the nerve center of the soul. It is strength. He gives anger to us so that we can fend off our passions, the devil. This is the correct use of anger. We take this strength from the

[6] Canon in this case means individual prayer by a monk in his cell determined by his superior.

devil and give it to Christ. You give yourself to Christ with strength, with nervous energy."

Did the Martyrs Feel Pain?

The Elder said to me, "There was a fellow here a little while ago who asked me if the martyrs felt pain during their torture? He was saying that God gave them patience and they endured the many tortures."

"To this I responded that, as a human being, one cannot stand pain. Neither could they stand the initial pain that they suffered. Naturally they ought to have fainted right away. But they focused their minds and their hearts on God.[7] 'Lord, Jesus Christ, have mercy on me. No, do not take pain away from me.' He knows the pain and allows it as much as is necessary to heal your soul."

"He sent you a specific penance instead of other types of penances. You should not ask that it be taken away. God knows your pain. A pill or some coffee is not needed. Do not use these things. Of course a person has the right in his life to ask, 'Dear God take the pain from me.' But I think that it is better for one to endure the pain. Probably this is a delusion but I love this delusion."

"Do not ask that penance be lessened. (In reality I had thought at that time that they lessen the number of

7 About overcoming pain from the martyrs' perspective the teaching of the Elder Porphyrios is analytically presented on pages 228-247 of the book of Const. Giannitsioti, "Near Elder Porphyrios".

prostrations I had to do. I was getting tired of having to do three hundred of them. "Struggle in whatever God has given you to do."

"How's your friend doing with the depression you were telling me about?"

"We took him to the doctor. He is giving him antidepressants. He is better now."

"Help him, my dear friend, to give himself to Christ with his whole heart- In this way he will overcome the depression and his nervous condition."

"Loving Christ with all our heart is most essential. This is where our entire effort should be directed."

Concerning His Cancer

The Elder said to me, "When I was younger I asked God to send me the illness of cancer so that I could suffer for His love. When I told it to my Elder, he said, 'No, this is egotism.' I therefore stopped asking for it.

'I sinned, Lord,' I was saying. Out of egotism I asked for something that was beyond my power to get. So now, after so many years, he sent me that which I asked for then. I have terrible pains."

"Elder, did you rejoice in it as when you asked for it or did it distress you?"

"When the doctors told me after they examined me I rejoiced and said, 'Glory to Thee O God. After so many years you did not forget my request.' I have cancer here in the pituitary gland. This has created a tumor that is growing and pressing upon the optic nerve. It was because of this that I was losing my sight.

"With this eye I see a little light. With the other I see the people like silhouettes but I cannot see details. My tongue has become thick and long. It creates a problem for me in my mouth and my voice has changed. I have dreadful pains. When I hurt, I am patient and I pray. When the pain is great, I cannot pray. However I don't make sounds nor do I complain."

"Elder, you should take a painkiller to reduce the pain."

"I don't take any. I say that which I told you, 'Doesn't Christ know that I am hurting?' He knows it. So I carry the Cross of Christ patiently.

"So, how does this look to you? I told you. They might call me crazy. However I like this craziness. I don't ask you to do the same. You can understand it as much as you can. That is the way I see it.

"I love you my dear man. Do you know it?"

"I know it, Elder. And I love you and ask through your prayers that God will have mercy on me."

"In my pain I ask God to have mercy on me and to forgive my sins. When man reaches the pre-fallen state God doesn't allow illness. And when it is His Will, we can immediately become healthy. These are difficult things to comprehend. Few are those to whom knowledge is given to understand them."

About Eating too much

I was present once when a lady called him and was asking the Elder to pray for her so that she would not eat too much. She had become fat. I was surprised by his answer.

"You have not loved Christ enough. Give your heart to Christ. Say with fervent love, Lord Jesus Christ, and you will forget the food and the gluttony will leave you."

I recorded this advice in my heart and when the opportunity was given I used it. I was once overcome with hunger before the scheduled meal I turned my thoughts to the prayer-Lord Jesus Christ, through the prayers of the Elder, have mercy on me. Without realizing it, my hunger went away until the scheduled time for the meal.

Some Healings
That He Himself Related To Me

"A little nun came to me who had a growth on her hand that was the size and shape of a walnut. When she showed it to me I said, "Let us go see the Professor." It was during the time that I was serving in the Polyclinic.

"I did not come to see the Professor" she said to me. "I came to see you."

I made the sign of the cross on her forehead, on her hand and sent her back to her monastery. She became well.

Another lady came to confession and while she was

confessing I discerned with the eyes of my soul that she had breast cancer.

"Are you well?", I asked her. "You have something."

"Yes, father, I am ashamed to say it."

"Go upstairs now and see this particular doctor and have him examine you. Then return to me to tell me what he said."

When she returned, she in fact had cancer. They had sent her for examinations and in three days she was going to be operated on. So when she returned I had her kneel with me.

"You say within yourself the Jesus Prayer," I told her. And I said the prayer. Afterwards I made the sign of the cross over her and sent her to do whatever the doctors said.

In three days when she returned for the operation, she was found well. There was no tumor or anything else. The doctor came down to the chapel to find me and he was quite beside himself.

"My beloved priest, what did you do to the woman that you made her well? If I had not touched the tumor with my hand and had not seen it with my eyes three days ago, I would not believe it."

The Elder continued, "My eyes see many things. I see very many miracles. The Grace of God acts on behalf of the faith of the people. You must believe that miracles also happen today because Christ is the same yesterday, today and unto the ages of ages."

Elder Do You Pray for All of the People You See Every Day?

Yes, I pray for everyone and even for those who leave without seeing me.

I pray for everyone in general. For some, however, I pray by name."

"Don't you get tired by so many people? How can you bear it?"

"I love them. I want to help everyone, but I can't and that upsets me. I talk constantly all day and my tongue gets dry. I start talking from 4 or 5 in the morning. In fact today an Abbot from the Holy Mountain called me at 5 in the morning, then a Bishop called me from Crete.

"The day before yesterday, at midnight, a father called from an island in the Pacific Ocean. Do you understand? While I am here, my spirit is also there. He told me about his daughters. I advised him about one of his daughters. The man rejoiced. I told him to call me again.

"When I get tired I cover my face and let them kiss only my hand. And they come, you know, from far away, from Alexandria the day before yesterday, from Kiato, from all parts of Greece and at other times from abroad. People come with serious problems. What can I do? I try. However I can't always speak. They get upset and they leave saying negative things about me.

"The Elder from the Paracletos [Monastery] tells me to accept them all. He said that I should say a few words to each one who comes or that everyone should at least get a blessing. You know one can't satisfy all the people. Today some might call me a Saint and tomorrow the reporters might write that I didn't satisfy the people or that I am a deceiver of the people."

His Food

One day, at noontime, I found myself standing near him.

The nuns told me that I would have to wait a little because it was time for his meal. "He must eat because it isn't good for him with an ulcer to remain on an empty stomach for many hours. And he has been talking to people since early this morning."

"Very gladly," I said, "I will wait here on the outside."

"Please call him to come inside," the Elder said. I entered.

"Sit here." I sat.

They brought him food. They brought an enameled plate with mashed, crushed food, a little napkin, and a spoon. Nothing else. The bread was hollowed out. They put the little napkin on him with loving care. They put the spoon in his hand, because he couldn't see at that time. Sitting he began putting the food into his mouth one bite at a time, maneuvering the spoon to his mouth with a trembling hand.

I was watching and yet I could not believe what I was seeing. I had seen in monasteries with what care they prepared the Abbot's food. There were plates, little plates, forks, and little forks, all precisely placed and exclusively all of them for the Abbot alone. Of course those who prepared these things did it out of love and dedication. But I also saw here an Orthodox spirit. I saw an ascetical, monastic spirit. I saw a spirit of Mount Athos. Everything was done simply, humbly and with holiness.

Because of my great surprise I don't know if I acted properly. I think that I told him, "Elder, do you want me to help you?" I was willing to feed him so that the food would not spill onto the little napkin.

"No, my child, thank you." He finished silently. He asked me for a glass of water which had been sitting on the firebrick stove.

"I have it there so that it can be kept warm for my neck." He washed out his mouth well. He wiped himself with the napkin. He rang the little bell and a nun came to take the plate.

"Elder, are you well? Maybe you desire something else?"

"No my child, thanks a-lot. Glory to thee O God." He did his cross many times as he had done also before he began, thanking God with his soul.

That which I experienced that noontime startled me more than any of the teachings of the Elder. I felt so humbled that God granted me, the unworthy one, an opportunity to see how a holy ascetic of the Holy Mountain eats, today in the 20th century, in Athens.

He told me about his food when he was suffering many pains from his ulcer. Later on he told me about the stomach hemorrhages caused by the cortisone shot for his eye. "I ate only mashed biscuits with a little wine. I couldn't even drink water. Now however I can."

About the Medicines

Elder, I often take medicines and I feel I am not acting right since you don't drink even coffee."

"I've told you about this on another occasion. When the Christian surrenders himself to trust in the Lord, it calms the internal organs. The result of this action is the normal functioning of the organs and the glands. As a consequence of this we enjoy good health and the absence of sickness. Because of sin, turmoil and egotism sometimes bring an increase or a decrease of good health with the consequent illnesses. The body knows that which is normal, that which is the middle road for good health. It responds with a sense of calmness and peace. For example, when I had the ulcer the doctor gave me this medicine. He showed it to me. It was Zantac. As soon as I took it, the pains immediately left me. Oh! I said. This is not good for it will have a side effect on some other part of my body. And I didn't take it again. I preferred to suffer the pain."

He kept asking me about a brother whom he knew.

"Elder," I told him, "he can't sleep at night and he is forced to take sometimes Stedon and other times Tranxen so that he can go to sleep."

"Tell him to come meet me here or to call me."

You Also Had to Help, Just a Little

Once when I went to meet him I had to wait outside for about an hour. All the people there were carrying bricks. They moved a few at a time a short distance away. I was waiting from moment to moment for them to call me. I was dressed in my Sunday clothes. I did not volunteer to offer a helping hand. When I went inside and I told him about this, he gave me some advice:

"You did not do well. You should have asked for an apron and sought permission to carry as many bricks as you could, even if just a few. This would have been beneficial to your soul and also to your body."

An Angry Brother

Another time, while I was speaking about another issue, he told me, "I see a brother who is very angry with you. He is like a beast ready to tear you to shreds." (And this was truly the case but I didn't want to say it).

"You are not to speak. We will pray and God will calm him down. Do you believe this?"

"I believe it."

"God alone changes the hearts of people. No matter what we do and how many things we say, we can accomplish nothing."

"But he, Elder, why does he do this? Why does he act in such a way, Elder?"

"Shh! Don't speak. It's not proper for me to tell you. You are to pray."

When Shall I Begin to Mourn?

Once I was very upset while I was waiting to be called so I could see the Elder. I was crying off to one side. As soon as I entered the Elder's cell, I found him sitting on his bed with his eyes closed. He could not see anything with his eyes. His hands were bandaged due to the infection which he was suffering.

"At what point shall I begin to mourn?" he said to me. He pulled me closer to him. He put my hand in his hands and for a long time he was silently counting my pulse. I believe that through this medical procedure, he imparted to me the Spirit of God through his fervent prayer. And as Christ did in performing His miracles by "touching the hand" of his patients, the Elder did the same.

You Fell, Give Yourself With Love to Christ

I recovered from my problem through what the Elder did. I was consoled and subsequently discussed my problem calmly with the Elder. He had read my heart completely.

"You are to blame for everything. You are sick in soul. You fell very low. You fell from your pure spiritual height. Do you understand this? You are to blame for everything. Just find the cause. Negligence? Egotism? From what you're saying, nothing is happening. Your fantasy is magnifying them. These problems are petty, very small and womanlike. Don't look at what others are doing. Look at your own self. How to love Christ.

"It is not your job to correct others. Let the Elder be concerned. You must pray for everyone. If they are doing wrong, pray that God enlighten them to correct themselves. These things are not corrected with words. They are only corrected with prayer. I see that you are influenced by others. Cut out drinking coffee. Forgive everyone with your heart. Pray fervently in your heart for everyone. Don't speak words. Don't speak. Do everything within yourself. You need introspection.

"I don't see that you have that divine love that you once had. Be careful in the beginning. Keep the first love that you had for the Lord. Retain the love and the divine affection that you had toward the Lord. It's not drowsiness that afflicts you but laziness.

"If we spoke a little on the phone, you would see that everything would immediately become resolved. Burden the body and don't fear the toil. Everything changes with hard work, both body and soul. Don't neglect the Jesus Prayer. Simply and without effort pray fervently for everyone. You will benefit them with prayer but not with words. If they ask your opinion, express it humbly, telling people that they may act as they please.

"Much prayer is needed. Embrace Christ with love and He will resolve all your problems. You must carry yourself with an air of simplicity and love. Because you have turned in upon yourself and have isolated yourself, you have forced others to isolate themselves from you and in the end they will think negatively of you. Now nothing is happening. Everything is a product of your fantasy. Believe me and give yourself with love to Christ. You fell a great deal and that is why all these things have affected you."

Don't Demand That Others Love You

D"istance yourself from jealousy. It eats up a person. A nun was angry with another nun because she imagined that she was saying bad things about her to the spiritual father. And she believed it was real. Everything happens to a jealous person. I have experienced this. People believe that I was good and many came to me for confession. These people spoke to me with great sincerity.

"Steer clear of female complaints. My dear friend we are to love Christ with passion, with divine love. Happy is the monk who has learned to love everyone spiritually. He doesn't seek love from others nor does it matter to him whether they love him or not.

"You are to love everyone and pray spiritually within yourself. Pour out your love towards everyone. And the time will come when you will love without effort. You will feel that everyone loves you. A secular song says:

"You asked me to love you
Love is not asked for
in the pages of the heart
it is born of its own self."

"Take it spiritually. You should radiate the love of Christ naturally. Some monastics, especially women monastics say, 'Do you love me? Why don't you love me?'

"My, my how far away they are from the love of Christ! This is poverty, spiritual poverty. Don't ever be concerned if they love you. You are to overflow with the love of Christ towards everyone. And mysteriously a change comes, a change for everything. That which I am telling you is the best missionary work possible. Implement it and call me with the results."

About Spiritual Silence

Y"our silence should be the mystery in your heart. Do not allow this spiritual A silence to show on the outside. Others should not be aware of it. As soon as you have said two or three words, continue spiritually to send prayers from within yourself for everyone to the Lord. Embrace within your heart the whole brotherhood and do this with love. Embrace the whole Church. Don't be anxious about anything nor try to solve or correct the faults of another. Love him with his faults. The Lord will take care of this.

Sanctify your silence with prayer so that it isn't barren and fruitless. "

About the Books of the Fathers

Study the fathers. They criticize the brotherhoods that function in the world that do not study the fathers. I worry that maybe you also hold such an opinion. At the refectory, study patristic texts related to the behavior between brothers. Read advisory works, i.e. Theodore, the Studite, Abba Dorotheos, and St. Ephraim the Syrian....

"Study the *Menaia*, the *Paracleteke* and the *Triodion*. There you will find ways to struggle, ways to overcome your faults in order to acquire virtue.

"The day before yesterday a fellow came here and asked me, 'Do you support the theories of such and such, - I didn't remember his name, - concerning the enjoyments of human pleasure and eros?'

I told him: 'There it is! What I support and what I maintain: Open the Menaion to June 14th the feast of Saint Methodios. There in the canon you will discover how Christ changes passion into calm.' I read it to him. I explained it to him and he was very pleased."

"You will find it as well, and when you do, call me."

I subsequently searched and this is what I found:

"Bridling the stirrings of passions by eros, (love of passion) of continence you transubstantiated the materialness of the flesh towards the mountain ridge of dispassion." [8]

(Ode 1, of Saint Methodius, June 14th).

"Christ does not uproot something that He has planted within us. He pricks it. He alters it from something that is wild to something that is tame. He turns it toward Christ and sanctifies it. Examples for us are,

[8] *"You Father bridling the stirrings of the passions, with the eros of continence you transubstantiated the material train of thought of the flesh (and you made it reach) the height of dispassion, O Father."*

Saint Mary of Egypt, Moses the Ethiopian, and many, many others."

You Got Badly Involved

A new brother came to the Monastery who became very close to me. He constantly asked for advice. He constantly told me what he did and when he was happy or when he was distressed.

"What can I do, Elder? If I scorn him he complains to the Elder. If I listen to him each time, I don't know if we are benefited."

"You have become badly involved. Now it is very difficult for you to get out of it. You can be helped only with prayer. He can't do without you. He needs two words in order for his soul to flourish again. The old type of monas- ticism doesn't exist any more. It has become unraveled. Friendships are not true and there is a desire to rule others. These types don't stay at the monastery. They don't bear fruit. In the end, with the slightest provocation they get up and leave."

And truly one year later, the brother left. He went to another monastery.

About Observation

I was distressed over certain observations and reprimands of me. I could not understand what I was doing wrong.

"But why, Elder Porphyrios, do they constantly scold me? For the slightest thing the monastery Elder scolds me. These observations come to me unexpectedly, suddenly, whereas I thought that I was doing well. I feel very sad and feel that I am being crushed. I have a fear that at any moment he will scold me again."

"My beloved, he is trying to save you and you complain about it? What are these things the Elder is telling you? You should have been there at Kavsokalyvia. Like you, once the thought about my parents possessed me. I missed them and I confessed it to my Elders.

The first time they asked me.

'How do you feel, my child?'

'Well, I am very pleased.'

'Yes, but you didn't ask us also, if we are pleased with you.'

'Forgive me, but I feel very happy and pleased. I pray to Christ that I become good so that you also will be pleased with me.'

While traveling I didn't have the permission to speak with anyone. The only thing I was allowed to say was bless and forgive[9], and I was on my way again. Later on I learned that they were very strict and no one could get along with them. Everyone would leave that place. To me they seemed good. In fact, I was distressed that I didn't have any problems. Once however, unexpectedly, a difficulty would come without my realizing it".

"How did this happen? Can you give me an example, please, so I can understand it?" I asked.

"I will tell you this now. One noontime I was in the

[9] Monastic greeting terminology.

kitchen. I finished my chores and then put some food on a large plate for the little cat and I went out to feed it. In a little while I went to enter but the door would not open for it was locked. I tried again but nothing happened. I saw Fr. Panteleimon on the inside of the door and he shouted loudly at me, 'Enter from there whence you came.'

"Not knowing what else to do, I went around and around with the plate in hand and came inside from the main entrance. 'As time passes by,' my Elder continued 'Instead of you improving and getting better, you are instead losing your mind. Have you forgotten where you came from? Did you not notice that the door is locked?'.

"I believed all of these things. I did not dare talk back. The only thing I kept saying was, 'Forgive me.'

"And within myself I kept saying: 'Lord, enlighten my darkness. My, my, how careless I am not to understand from whence I came...' And during the course of many days in doing chores, I proclaimed with pain within myself: 'Lord, enlighten my darkness.' Now, however, in pondering these things, I have understood that it was a type of training for me as a novice monk. They wanted to see if I would get angry, if I would talk back or if I could be cultivated in humility.

"You know, my child, we are not always ready when we ask something from God, like humility, for example. When we are mature He gives it to us. We must have the eyes of our soul open so that we understand His purpose. God hides in the darkness. 'From the brightness before His thick clouds passed[10],' it says in a particular psalm. Have you seen it?"

"Yes, I heard it, but I did not comprehend the deep meaning of this verse. Now that you are saying this to me my soul is elated. It is leaping with joy."

"Of course God hides so that He may protect us in humility. He helps us do the good and then He hides. He envelopes us also so that we don't understand. Look and see if you can find that particular psalm and then call me to tell me about it. The more one does good, the more he becomes one with it and he can no longer do evil. Even if he wants to, he cannot. Do you understand this?"

"May God enlighten me to understand all these things that you are telling me."

"But it is good for me to draw near to God." [11]

"Attachment means being nailed to the Cross, to the Lord. To be crucified with the Lord is everything. It is like the metal that is being forged in the fire. Iron and fire become one but when the iron comes out of the fire it becomes iron again. Man becomes subject to the fall through the envy of the devil. A mystical Pascha! Let us mystically celebrate. The plan of God from all time is fulfilled for our salvation."

"May we be impressed upon You." [12]

[10] Psalm 17:12

[11] For it is good for me to draw near to God (Psalm 72:28)

[12] "More carved let us participate in You" (like the seal is imprinted on the prosforon thus let us be imprinted in You, that is to get Your

"Types of prophets and riddles." [13]

"Don't think that when we die we will go there to rejoice, to feel the goodness of God. We must feel it from here. If we don't unite with Him from here and we are not crucified with Christ we will neither be with Him there.

"Paradise is not a place filled with beautiful fruit-bearing trees, flowers, etc. It is the spiritual happiness that the soul feels in God. What I am telling you now is expressed in a hymn that I like to quote.

'I am prosperous in aromas but poor in virtues. That which I have, I offer it to You. Give yourself of what you have and I will forgive you the adulteress cries out to Christ.' [14]

"It is taken from the 9th ode of the Triodion, the Canon of St. Andrew of Crete which is read on Holy Tuesday, during the Compline).

"Search that you may find it where it is written. In either case, you will find it in the Triodion.

"Read the *Menaia*, the *Paracleteke*, *Triodion*, and the *Pentecostarion*. You will find much wealth there."

character). The verse is from the troparion of the 9lh ode of the Sunday of Pascha.

13 Prophecies of the prophets and their enigmatic words are implemented and explained in the person of Christ.

14 "I am rich in aromas but poor in virtues. That which I have I offer to you. You give that what you have and forgive me proclaims the fornicating woman to Christ". It is from the 9'' old of the Canon in the Triodion of Andrew of Crete, which is read on Holy Tuesday at the Compline.

About Physical Effort

Once I complained to Elder Porphyrios that I couldn't stand it any more. We did so many chores during those days that "we became exhausted" I told him, "I don't have the strength to lift my feet and my hands. Why are so many chores needed in a Monastery?"

He became very serious and answered directly,

"It is a mortal sin for us to get tired of God to repent, and then to complain.

"Understand it well. Without physical labor virtue cannot be achieved. Nothing is gained by lying in bed.

"Physical labor is the greatest gift of God for our salvation. It is the greatest gift given to us so that we may obtain grace from God.

"The others accepted, with joy, humiliations and toils... and you are suffering?

"The greatest sin is while we are toiling for Christ, to feel sorry for ourselves and to suffer.

"My good man, you a young man, and you say that you get tired? When I was your age I flew. I wanted to complete everything. Don't look at me now that I can't do anything."

"I see that you are very much slower than the others. The old person in you took over and you have been crushed. NO! Recover your strength! Chant the tone with fervor and joyously!"

"We celebrate the death of death
The abolition of Hades
We begin the other life of the eternal.

And leaping we proclaim the cause.
The only blessed one of the Fathers, God
and most glorious."

He chanted it beautifully, clearly, and with meaning (all this on the telephone). He told me that I should also say it and so I did. I began saying it. "Not like that. Say it with meaning, clearly, word by word." He had me say it three times. "Learn it well and call me again to say it to me again."

I did whatever he told me without giving it a second thought. I wondered why he was telling me this or that. Whatever he told me I believed without reservation. I implemented it and immediately my inner being changed. I was resurrected. I gained new strength. I did my chores with such eagerness. It was as if the Elder was next to me and shared my work with me. On that particular day he told me the following event that happened while he was living in the Skete.

"With the grace of God I never broke a glass or a plate. I washed them with lye. We didn't have any soap. I did everything quickly and well. I was focused, quick, eager, precise and obedient. I do not say these things out of egotism but for the glory of God. I had holy elders. Do you remember how it is said in the Odes that we can boast but only in the Lord.

He allowed me to think and later he said it himself:
"In this let the boasting person boast,
(in the) understanding and knowing the Lord..."
"Go find it and study it."

We Should Pray With Our Eyes Open

He told me, "Let us pray with open eyes." I asked, "why Elder can't we pray with closed eyes?" He responded, "We are not dealing with hypnotism here my child. And I, whenever I pray to help a soul or a person I pray with open eyes. Whatever the Spirit says to me, I say. Whatever it reveals to me, this I say."

When He Began To Go To His Hermitage

As I have told you many times, my great desire is to close my eyes (die) at the monastery of my repentance there on the Holy Mountain. What concerns me always is how my body will get used to that climate so that I can bear it. So I found a beautiful place in Evia that has the same climate as that of the Holy Mountain. What can I tell you about it? My soul opens up there. My lungs feel good. J feel the joy of God! I began going there one day a week and stayed here six days. Later I would go there for two days and stay five here. Slowly, very slowly I will increase the days until I become acclimatized. What do you think? Is it possible that I am deceiving myself?" I was overwhelmed with his plan and with his humility. "How do you get along there, Elder? Where do you stay?"

"How can I explain it to you! Anyone who hears it will think that we have gone crazy. I live in the car. This place is wild. There are rocks, forests and birds." (And it should be noted that, at this time, he was completely blind). "At night I take my walk. It is cold. I take a bottle with warm water with me and keep it near my chest. This keeps me warm. And thus I jump from rock to rock and do my spiritual exercises. I rejoice in prayer. No one bothers me. I think that I am on the Mountain. You know from that corner of Evia, when the horizon is clear the peninsula of the Holy Mountain comes into view. I don't have the heart to leave that place."

A Little Later: I Went to Him Mentally and Told Him....

"Nowdays my legs have a tendency to go numb and they don't allow me to walk. I only take a few steps. I forget easily. I don't ask God to make me well. I only ask Him to forgive my sins. I often think of you and pray for you saying the prayer for you: 'Lord Jesus Christ, have mercy on me.' Feel free to call me often."

"Elder, the day before yesterday I was very upset and since you were absent what could I do? I said I would communicate with you from afar".

"And you came and knelt at my feet, is that right?"

"Yes, Elder, it is exactly as you say it."

I was startled at this revelation.

"Truly, in my pain I went to my cell. I knelt with the sense that I was before the bed of the Elder kneeling and told him of my pain. 'My dear Christ,' I said in the end, 'please inform him to pray for me, he who has great courage.' Truly, in a short time I came out as a new person. Now it was verified to me that the Elder had full knowledge of my actions and my problems."

The Same Thing Happened To Me Even After His Repose

When I was having a difficult time and not knowing where to turn to for help, I suddenly thought of Elder Porphyrios and I knelt in my cell and prayed.

"My Lord Jesus, please inform the good Elder about my problem. His grave is too far away for me to speak to him. But here, I am psychically near him.

"My dear Holy Father, I have this problem that is afflicting me. Please help me in your usual manner. You know how to handle it. You can do much more now that you are near to Christ. You can do more now than before your death. I'm not asking you 'to take away' the difficulties but to arm me with spiritual strength."

I got up from this prayer of mine with renewed strength, the same strength that I used to feel when I left his cell.

I thanked God who glorifies those who glorify Him.

Nightly Telephone Conversations With the Holy Mountain

He spoke to me about the monks from his hut on the Holy Mountain. They would call him at night and speak to him for many hours about spiritual matters and they would be very thankful.

"They are compiling material from the Holy Scriptures, from hymnology and from the fathers on mystical theology, mystical life and the union of the soul with God. When they find these passages they tell me about them and my soul rejoices."

'Theotokos you are a Mystical Paradise'.

'I shall dwell among them and walk in them (2 Cor. 6: 16).

'I see a mystery odd and strange'

'I mystically receive knowledge that has been commanded.'

'The angelic powers wondered at that which happened in You, O immaculate one...'

'I wonder and am amazed' 'Every one was startled at the ineffable condescension of God'

'The universe was surprised by Your divine glory'

'Being fired up by the warmth of love for Christ, unconsumed by fire the contestants remained inside the fire, setting fire to the thorns of impiety by Divine Grace.'

He loved to memorize these and other things and to carry on conversations with the monks of his Skete.

About the Takeover of Cyprus

During one of our conversations he mentioned to me the following:

"I was headed to the Holy Mountain with a particular person, I don't quite remember his name.

On the way towards Thessalonica, I suddenly told him to stop. We got out of the car. I asked him to draw a map of Cyprus. He took a stick and drew a map of Cyprus in the sand. I then drew a line through Cyprus and divided it.

'You see here,' I told him. 'At this very moment the Turks are fiercely invading Cyprus and are cutting up the Cypriots. Much blood is being shed. Let's pray.'

"We stopped there for a long time and prayed. I suffered a lot because through the grace of God and at that very moment I was living all the drama of those people.

"It was with a great deal of difficulty I was able to continue our trip. Later on I learned that they wrote these things in the newspapers and announced them on the radio.

You can see from this that the Spirit of God blows wherever it so desires"[15].

About My Tonsure

He told others as he also told me that he was spiritually present at my tonsure as a monk. While doing this he was physically sick in his cell. He had seen and observed everything through this gift of Grace that he had received from

[15] The event is also mentioned in the book of Kl. Ioannides, *The Elder Porphyrios* 7th edition, page 141. Small differences in the narration are due to the imperfection of the human memory of those who are making the documentation. The essential thing is that the Elder saw with his clairvoyance the invasion of Cyprus.

God. During the week I was cloistered in silence and prayer, I intensely felt his presence. When later on I told him about this, he assured me, that truly he was spiritually near me and observed my spiritual journey during those days.

Only One Day a Week at Milessi

During his last days, he spoke with great joy about the Holy Mountain. "From now on, I stay at Milessi only one day a week. The rest of the time I spend it at my hermitage. I think that I have gotten used to the climate. In a little while I will leave for the Skete of my repentance. Good and spiritual monks are waiting for me there. May God grant me the privilege to finish my life there."

"Won't the sisters here, who love you so much, be distressed?"

"If their love is human they will get distressed.

"When our love is in Christ, we want that which the person we love desires. I have received notification from Christ that He wants me to return to the Monastery of my Repentance."

His Heart Is A Divine Abyss

He told me, "God has given you so many gifts. He adorned you with rare gifts. Do you feel this? Thank Him constantly and humble yourself for His Love.[16]

"Ask God to send you blessed humility. Not the type of humility that says, I am least of all, I am worthless. This is satanic humility. Blessed humility is a gift of God. Do you hear me? It is a gift. It is a gift from God. It does not come from our own efforts. Prepare yourself and seek this Holy Gift from God. Don't say that I have this fault and I offer it to God. You are to say nothing. You should struggle and put yourself down and all the other things are from God.

"Struggle beginning here so that we can enter the uncreated church of God.

"When you pray, don't pray only for your own self. Saying 'Lord Jesus Christ, have mercy on me, you should feel the whole monastic brotherhood next to you, the whole Church in every corner of the earth, the struggling, living, Orthodox Church.

"You should also pray for our triumphant and perfected Church. We are all one in God including all who will come after us and unto the close of the age."

When the Elder was telling me these things he made

16 This seems like praise but it is not. The Elder here is not referring to special gifts which God gives to the charis- matics, but to gifts of life, health, education, monastic calling etc. which God granted to the person with whom He was conversing.

me feel like an abyss of ignorance. It made me feel as if I knew nothing.

"But I am in the bosom of the Omniscient and All-greatness of God. And here is where we understand the meaning of the abysmal *abyss* of the psalmist. We also understand here the meaning of *'Lord, conceal me in Your darkness, in Your divine cloud'*.

"Because the Psalmist says (Psalm 17: 10: 12), 'He made darkness his secret place; his canopy around Him were dark waters and thick clouds of the skies.'

The Elder repeated this often. He said it with meaning in a way that moved my soul every time. Who knows how he lived this experience. I made notes of all these things and I pass on these holy words of our Holy Father. I only pray that I will never forget them but that I will live them for as long as I live.

His Appointment to the Polyclinic

I will now tell you what he himself related to me in relation to his appointment to the Polyclinic of Athens. I will tell you the difficulties that he first encountered. I will describe them simply just the way he told them to me in his descriptive, narrative manner.

I left this part for last because I found it published elsewhere and it is known.

He related these things to me in order to teach me that there are always ways for us to overcome difficulties when we give our heart to Christ.

His narrative was given in a joyous and vigorous tone. This is when I first met him.

"Now listen to what I have to tell you, "When I went to Athens, I wanted very much to work with sick people. I searched to find a hospital that had an opening for a chaplain.

"That is when I found the Polyclinic. But it was difficult, as you may understand, because I did not have a degree in theology.

"I went and found Professor Alivizato in his office. He listened to me attentively and responded to my request by saying, 'But I want a priest who is a theologian to work in the Clinic. How can this be?' he asked. 'I do not know how to give talks,' I told him. 'But I know how to read and I will perform the liturgy. Give me a chance and you will see that you will be well pleased.'

'Would you tell me how many books are in the New Testament he asked me?'

'Twenty-seven, I answered him. The four gospels, the Acts of the Apostles, the fourteen epistles of Paul, the seven catholic epistles and the Revelation of John.'

'Bravo! Super! Go and I will give you an answer.'

Truly the Professor was well pleased. I don't know, it may be possible that people from the Archdiocese intervened and that is why they appointed me."

The Muffling of the Sounds

H"owever, from the first Liturgy that I 'attempted to perform, I encountered great difficulty."

"What difficulty did you encounter?"

"Specifically, outside of the entrance of the Church was a little shop that sold records. In order to advertise his records, the storekeeper had a record player on which he played music. From morning until night he played erotic songs as loud as possible.

"Just think for a moment. While I was saying *'Again and many times we fall down before Thee,* outside the erotic words were being heard.

"I suffered greatly because of this. I was saying to myself what can I do? It's impossible for me to continue under these conditions. I must leave here and give up. But I was ashamed because of the professor to whom I had pleaded so much to get this position."

"Why didn't you tell the person who was creating the problem? You could ask him in a nice way to stop the music during the Liturgy."

"I went and found him. I introduced myself and told him that I was the new priest and I was not used to these sounds. I told him that maybe he could, at the time of the Liturgy, play the music softer."

'What are you saying to me, priest? he replied. If I don't sell them on Sunday when will I sell them in order to make a living? You do your job and I will do my job.'

"Finally I decided to entrust the whole issue to God. I decided that I would pray and fast for three days. And I would ask God to reveal to me in a clear and simple way what I must do. Should I stay or leave?

'My God', I told Him, 'reveal to me in a simple way, so that I can understand what I must do.'

"I suffered a lot because of this. During the next Liturgy the answer came to me in a way I could have never imagined."

I, filled with wonder, looked in the eyes of the Elder trying to guess how God answered his prayer.

"At the next Liturgy, a student of the Polytechnic School came[17] and helped me in the Altar.

"We finished and upon leaving the student forgot his physics notes. I, curious as I was, took and read them with much interest.

"The notes were about sound waves, the smaller and the larger ones. It described how the larger waves negate the smaller ones and mask them. They wrote about other important things that I interpreted spiritually. Through divine grace, at that very moment, as I was reading these notes, I received an answer to my problem. I was filled with joy and rejoicing.

'Eureka!' I shouted like Archimedes, 'eureka!' The record player sends sound waves into the atmosphere.

"I will also send larger waves to God, of a stronger intensity and they will cover the sound waves from the record. They will wipe out the waves put out by the record player and they will vanish.

"So, on the next Sunday, I implemented the plan. I focused all my mind and heart on the words of the prayers. I said them with strength of soul. I did this even with the silent prayers. I tell you sincerely that I didn't hear anything else. This Liturgy was the most beautiful of my life. I lived in another world. And I thanked God

[17] Now he's a dentist.

a lot, because He so simply and decisively gave me an answer to my problem.

Thus I stayed at the Polyclinic."

"Fine, Elder, you were able to overcome this problem. What about the people who attended Church, weren't they bothered by the music?"

"They were used to the noises of Athens and it didn't bother them.

"I, on the other hand, had been trained in the quiet of the wilderness and now found myself suddenly in the midst of bedlam. Do you understand me?

"They were not bothered. I was bothered. But by the grace of God, in the subsequent Liturgies also, God continued to envelope me and I was not bothered. This went on until God enlightened this man with the music and he came to his senses. In a short time the record player was turned off at the time of the Liturgy.

"Furthermore he came and found me and he expressed his sadness that he had disturbed me.

"I want you to understand also that no problem exists without a solution in Christ. Give yourself to Christ and He will find you a solution.

"Don't fear difficulties[18]. Love them and thank God for them. They have some holy purpose for your soul."

[18] Recall whatever is written above related to the love of temptations (page 38).

Advice for Pregnant Mothers

He told a pediatrician. "Tell mothers to feel how much God has honored them. He has granted them the privilege to become mothers. From the moment that they carry within themselves the conceived embryo, they carry a second life.

"They should speak to their child. They should caress it by rubbing its stomach. The embryo feels these things spiritually.

"They should pray with much love for the embryo. But on the contrary not only does an infant feel things but also the embryo feels the lack of his mother's love. It feels her nervousness. It feels her anger. It feels her aversions. These things wound the little soul that remains with that person throughout their whole life.

"The spiritual emotions and life of the mother sanctifies her child even from the time of its conception.

The same is also true for the father."

Advice to a Pediatrician

He asked the same pediatrician, "How do you examine the children?" "In this manner... the pediatrician replied"

"Listen to what I have to say to you. Every time you examine a child you should offer a fervent prayer with love: 'Lord Jesus Christ, have mercy on your servant'.

As he said these things he took a deep breath while he opened his hands.

"It is in this way that you should pray for every child. God has sent a precious little soul into your hands.

"As you place your hand on their little heads pray fervently within yourself that the grace of God will be transfused into the soul of the child.

"Do all these things spiritually and in secret. The others who are present won't understand anything.

"You will prescribe to them medicines which science dictates, but in the final analysis Christ will heal the child. You and the parents desire this. Do you believe this?"

Another time he said to the same pediatrician. "I don't see you examining the children the way I had told you. The routine is getting to you and you are forgetting. My dear man, give yourself to Christ and offer these little creatures to Christ with your prayer so that you can sanctify them!

"Did you see, Christ healed by using the sense of touch? He either touched their hands, or touched their eyes, or the tongue. You will do the same thing.

"You will embrace the little child or you will hold the hand of the older one. And with the intense and fervent prayer to Christ you will infuse the grace of God in them. Doesn't the priest also do the same thing in every sacrament?

"In order for the grace of the Holy Spirit to come, he places his hand on the head of the person who seeks penance. He does the same thing for a person getting married or a person who is getting baptized etc.

"Prayer is spiritual power that is imparted spiritually to the other person's soul."

Others Who Knew His Life

When I asked him about his life he said, "Everything about me is known by Father such and such[19] and a few others. After my death they will acquaint you with them all. Now I have told you enough."

He Saw Everything

When I told him about the first Liturgy that took place at a monastery with a vigil he said to me, "I know everything. Through the grace of God I observed everything that happened from here where I was.

"Especially Father such and such was most ecstatic. He was completely beside himself. It was a Liturgy that pleased God."

[19] We don't mention his name so that he's not troubled by a flood of questions.

"Death does not exist. Don't fear death"

PRAYER

And may our life,
through the prayers of Elder Porphyrios,
be a total Liturgy which pleases God
Amen.

Printed in Great Britain
by Amazon

49429787R00061